Let's see, how does our garden grow?
With seeds that sprout all in a row.

To grow from seeds is lots of fun.
Just add soil, rain and sun.

We learn it's quite incredible that parts of plants are edible!

There are some roots we like to eat, onion, carrot, and a beet.

Some other food comes from leaves, like lettuce, spinach & collard greens.

Let's grow tomatoes for a start.
We'll watch them grow
and all take part.

When they're ripe we pick a bunch.
They end up being in our lunch!

Grow it, eat it, hey, who knew?
It's fun to eat the foods we grew!

We visit farms close by our town and see food growing all around.

Farms send food to markets & schools which we enjoy and find so cool.

More "local" foods are always great.
They reach us faster on our plate.